Read All About Whales

THE WHALES' WORLD

Jason Cooper

The Rourke Corporation, Inc.
Vero Beach, Florida 32964

© 1996 The Rourke Corporation, Inc.

All rights reserved. No part of this book may be reproduced or utilized in any form or by any means, electronic or mechanical including photocopying, recording or by any information storage and retrieval system without permission in writing from the publisher.

PHOTO CREDITS
©Brandon Cole: p.9, 20; ©Doug Perrine/INNERSPACE VISIONS: p.10, 19, 22; ©Lynn M. Stone: cover, p.12, 13; ©©James D. Watt/ INNERSPACE VISIONS: p.16; ©Ken Bondy/INNERSPACE VISIONS: p.18; Peter Howorth: p.6, 15; ©Thomas Kitchin: p.4; ©Tom Campbell: p.7

Library of Congress Cataloging-in-Publication Data

Cooper, Jason, 1942-
    The whales' world / by Jason Cooper
      p. cm. — (Read all about whales)
    Includes index.
    Summary: Describes the behavior of whales, with an emphasis on their hunting, communication and travel.
    ISBN 0-86593-449-5
    1. Whales—Juvenile literature. [1. Whales.]
I. Title II. Series: Cooper, Jason, 1942-   Read all about whales
QL737.C4C655 1996
599.5—dc20   96–19189
                                                        CIP
                                                        AC

Printed in the USA

TABLE OF CONTENTS

The Whales' World 5

Predator and Prey 6

The Marine World 8

How Whales Hunt 11

Echolocation 12

Whale Talk 14

Whales at Sea 17

Whale Travel 18

Whale Senses 20

Glossary 23

Index 24

THE WHALES' WORLD

They look like fish. They swim like fish. They even share the fish's saltwater world. But whales and their smaller cousins, the porpoises and dolphins, are **mammals** (MAM uhlz). Like all mammals, whales breathe fresh air and grow up on mother's milk.

Nearly the entire family of whales lives in the seas, shallow and deep, warm and cold. The few that do not live in seawater—a group of dolphins—live in rivers.

They look fishlike and live in the fish's world, but whales are air-breathing mammals.

PREDATOR AND PREY

The whales' **marine** (muh REEN), or saltwater, world is home to **predators** (PRED uh terz) and **prey** (PRAY). Predators are hunting animals. Their prey is what they catch. All whales are meat eaters, so they are all hunters.

A huge blue whale, the largest animal on Earth, gulps shrimplike krill from the sea.

Toothed whales, like these spotted dolphins, live mostly on fish and squid.

The big **baleen** (buh LEEN) whales don't have teeth. Instead their upper jaws have several rows of comblike baleen. These whales eat small animals that the baleen filters out of the sea.

The toothed whales live mostly on a diet of fish and squid.

THE MARINE WORLD

Whales need animal food, but they also need sunlight and marine plants for their well-being.

Marine plants grow by turning sunlight into food. The plants then feed a whole parade of marine animals. Some of the plant eaters become meals for predators.

Whales are part of the marine web of plants and animals. Each strand of the web is connected to the other.

Living in the marine world requires a special design for whales, such as flippers.

A humpback whale's baleen strains small fish from seawater.

HOW WHALES HUNT

Baleen whales trap small marine animals in their mouths. Using their tongues, the whales force huge mouthfuls of water through the baleen "combs."

Toothed whales are true hunters. They attack squid and schools of fish. Often they target schools of fish they can't even see!

Sunlight cannot reach the deep water where some whales hunt. So how can toothed whales find food? They use **echolocation** (EK o lo KAY shun), just as bats do.

In deep, dark water, sperm whales and other toothed whales turn on their echolocation systems.

ECHOLOCATION

Bats and whales live in worlds far apart. Both have to hunt in darkness, however. Both need a way other than eyesight to find food.

Nature solved their problem with echolocation. Whales and bats send out sound waves. The sound bounces back an echo when it strikes an object.

Echolocation allows these killer whales to swim apart but stay in touch with each other and with food.

Humpback whales sometimes communicate with each other by flipper-slapping the ocean's surface.

A whale can tell a whole lot about what's in an area by "reading" the echo. Even in a world of darkness, a whale can echolocate a meal.

WHALE TALK

Sound travels well underwater. Whales send out many different sounds to locate each other in the distance and darkness. Their calls probably help them communicate moods and other information.

Some whales talk to each other with chirps, clicks, or moans. Humpback whales make a long series of notes that are called "songs." Each humpback sings a song much like every other humpback. Scientists aren't sure why humpbacks sing.

Humpbacks make mysterious music undersea—and fantastic leaps above.

WHALES AT SEA

Large whales generally swim quite slowly. The fin whale is the fastest of the big whales. It can swim 12 miles per hour. Smaller whales are much faster. Certain porpoises can zip along at up to 35 miles per hour.

Many whales swim close to the sea surface, where they feed. Others are deep divers, feeding on animals near the ocean bottom. The great sperm whale can dive to more than a mile deep!

The great whales usually swim slowly and with little effort through their sea world.

WHALE TRAVEL

The ocean world changes with the seasons. Oceans become cooler or warmer. Food becomes plentiful, and it becomes scarce.

Many whales travel with their source of food. The large baleen whales generally spend winter in warm seas and summers in cold waters.

The gray whale's sea world changes as it travels south in autumn, north in spring.

Whales like to bear their calves in warm seas.

Cold seas have the greatest amount of **plankton** (PLANK ton). Plankton is a stew of small, floating marine creatures. Baleen whales live on the plankton they sift from the ocean water.

Baleen whales travel up to 3,000 miles each way on their journeys.

Toothed whales travel, too, but usually not great distances.

WHALE SENSES

Whales neither have, nor need, great eyesight. In the dark undersea world, hearing is far more important.

A whale depends upon its ability to hear well. Sound helps a whale find food and other whales. It is also an important way for whales to communicate with each other.

Whales have a keen sense of touch, too. That helps them identify food and perhaps each other.

Whales seem to have no sense of smell.

A whale's eyesight is poor. By poking its head out, a gray whale takes a closer look around the air world above.

GLOSSARY

baleen (buh LEEN) — the tough, comblike plates found in the upper jaws of certain whales; whalebone

echolocation (EK o lo KAY shun) — a whale's system of using echoes to locate food and its surroundings underwater

mammals (MAM uhlz) — the group of air-breathing, warm-blooded, milk-producing animals

marine (muh REEN) — of or relating to the ocean

plankton (PLANK ton) — tiny floating plants and animals of the sea and other bodies of water

predators (PRED uh terz) — animals that hunt other animals for food

prey (PRAY) — an animal that is hunted by another animal for food

Whales have a keen sense of touch. These sperm whales are rubbing against each other. Touch helps whales communicate.

INDEX

baleen 7
bats 11, 12
dolphins 5
echolocation 11, 12
fish 7, 11
flippers 8
food 8, 11, 12, 20
mammals 5
plankton 19
plants, marine 8
porpoises 5, 17
predators 6, 8
prey 6
rivers 5

seas 5, 18
senses 20
songs 14
squid 7, 11
sunlight 8, 11
tongues 11
whales 5, 6, 8, 12, 14, 17, 18, 19, 20
  baleen 7, 11, 18
  fin 17
  humpback 14
  sperm 17
  toothed 7, 11, 19